AF507173

Welcome to Jackson Hole, Teton Valley, our majestic Teton mountains, and the beautiful Grand Teton and Yellowstone National Parks. We offer your children a coloring book to allow their imaginary views come to life, drawing on a spectrum of colors as they see in nature while reinforcing the alphabet.

While your family visits the Valley, may your days be filled with long–term memories and pleasant adventures. May you enjoy our enchanting Summer, and metamorphosis of our golden yellow Fall, and the chilly, exhilarating days of Winter. We hope you love these mountains as much as we do.

Mountain Love,
Kris and Julie

ABC's of JACKSON HOLE

WRITTEN BY: KRISTIN POOLE

ILLUSTRATED BY: JULIE MILLARD

First paperback edition April 2024
ISBN: 979-8-3507-3088-3

About the Author:
Kristin loves the mountains, especially the Tetons.
When she first moved to Jackson and looked out
the car window, gazing at the Grand Teton,
she was speechless which does
not happen often. She combined her
love of Jackson and her love of books
to fuel this project.

About the Illustrator:
Julie grew up in the shadow of the Tetons.
She has explored many of the canyons
and trails in these beautiful mountains.
She loves to draw and paint the
mountains, the animals, and the people
that make this place home.

ANTLER ARCHES

The antler arches are on the Town Square. The local Boy Scouts collect antlers from the National Elk Refuge in May. How many antlers do you think are in each arch? It is estimated to be about 8,000 elk antlers total, in all four arches. People who visit Jackson often take their picture under the arch. Local music groups play under the arches at the Farmer's Market. During the holiday season the arches are wrapped in twinkling lights.

BISON, BEARS, BIRDS, BEAVERS

Jackson is known for wildlife. Bring binoculars to look for birds and other animals. Birds such as osprey and bald eagles are frequently spotted. Often the bison are grazing close to the road, so you don't even need binoculars to see them! Take a scenic raft float and wildlife may be grazing and moving along the water's edge.

A family camping trip is an experience to remember! Cooking over a campfire under the stars is so fun! S'mores are a tasty, sticky, gooey treat. Snuggle into your sleeping bag and enjoy a book or coloring by flashlight.

DOGS

Dogs are family in Jackson Hole! Dogs are adventure partners, whether hiking Snow King, or swimming, we love our furry family. Some dogs have special jobs such as dogs on sledding teams, avalanche dogs, and dogs working on ranches.

Jackson is home to the amazing National Elk Refuge. In the winter elk migrate to the refuge. Visit the National Elk Refuge Visitor's center to take a sleigh ride out to see the elk up close. They conserve their energy in the winter by inhabiting the refuge. In the warmer months they migrate to the surrounding mountains.

FLY FISHING

Fly fishing is a sport that combines the skill of mind and body. It involves learning how to tie knots, hike the terrain for the perfect spot, or hop on a drift boat to explore new waters in pursuit of a tug on the line. That tug means a fish has grabbed a fly!

There are many creeks to explore around Jackson. The creeks are home to fish such as cutthroat, rainbow, brown, and brook trout. Often you will see anglers wading in the water hoping for a bite.

GATHERING

Jackson Hole is a wonderful place for Gathering! Families and friends gather here to explore the outdoors for weddings and family reunions.

HIKING

Hiking trails are all over. The views around Jackson as you hike are breathtaking. Capture the beauty of the mountains and the fresh air when you hike. Use your senses as you explore: What do you hear? What do you smell? What can you touch? What do you see?

INDIGENOUS PEOPLES

Native American Indians are the earliest inhabitants. There are over ten indigenous tribes who lived in the area.

JACKSON HOLE

Jackson Hole is the name of the valley between the Teton Range and the Snake River. Early trappers called it a 'hole' because of the steep slope they traveled down to trap and hunt.

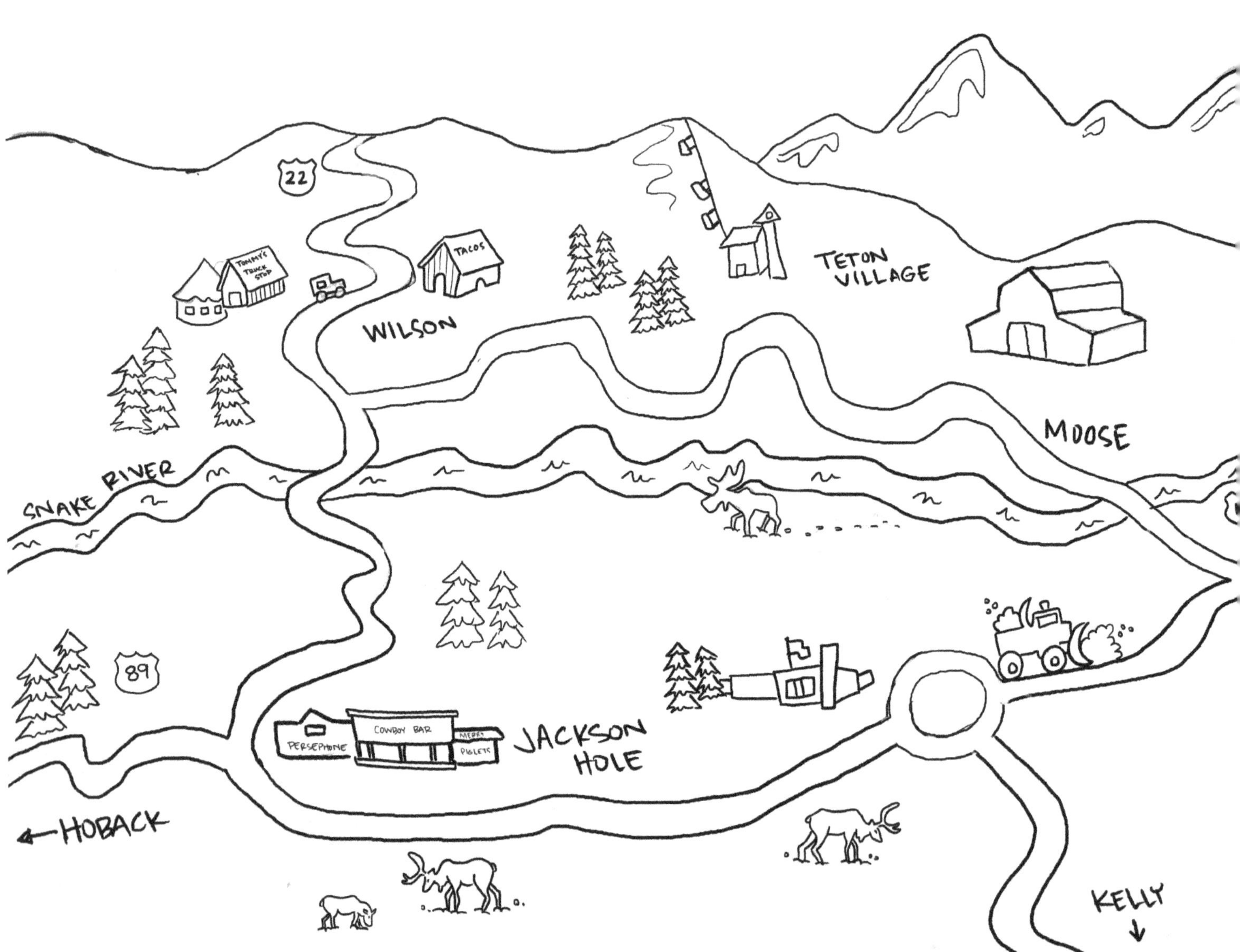

There are so many fun things for kids to do in Jackson Hole and Teton Valley. Exploring, running, hiking, skiing, biking, rafting, fishing, laughing and gazing at the mountains are all fun activities for kids to do. It's like a giant playground.

LAKES

Lakes around Jackson include Jackson Lake, String Lake, Leigh Lake, Phelps Lake, and Jenny Lake to name a few. The lakes are a great place to take a picnic or swim. Water sports including paddle boarding, kayaking, and canoeing are some of the most fun for families to enjoy. Jenny Lake is in Grand Teton National Park and was formed by glaciers thousands of years ago. There is a scenic boat trip around the lake, or you can walk around Jenny Lake and up to Hidden Falls and Inspiration Point. Jenny Lake has trails that lead to climbing the tallest peaks of the Teton Range.

Moose are part of the deer family. The males have antlers, and the females are very protective of their young. They love to eat willows and are often seen in Wilson along the roadside. Remember to stay far back and just observe them with your eyes and take a picture. Moose are wild so you want to give them distance to roam and eat.

NATURE

Nature is the natural world around us. For many, exploring in nature is a mindful experience. In the summer wildflowers bloom. The Indian Paintbrush is the Wyoming State Flower; it's red and looks like a paintbrush.

OPEN RANGE

Cattle and horses graze in open range.
They can be free to run, graze, and roam.

PASS

The Pass, or Teton Pass, is the road that connects Wyoming and Idaho. The elevation at the top is 8,431 feet! It is the perfect place to backcountry ski or snowmobile in the serenity of the terrain. Take a picture in front of the sign that says, 'Howdy Stranger, Yonder is Jackson Hole: The Last of the Old West'. There are other iconic mountain passes such as Togwotee Pass and Sylvan Pass in Yellowstone.

QUIET STARRY NIGHT

Look up at the starry night sky! Do you see all the stars in the quiet darkness? They glisten and sparkle, the color around them so dark. The Teton Range will seem to change colors as the sun sets each day and rises each morning. Wish upon a star for another trip to Jackson.

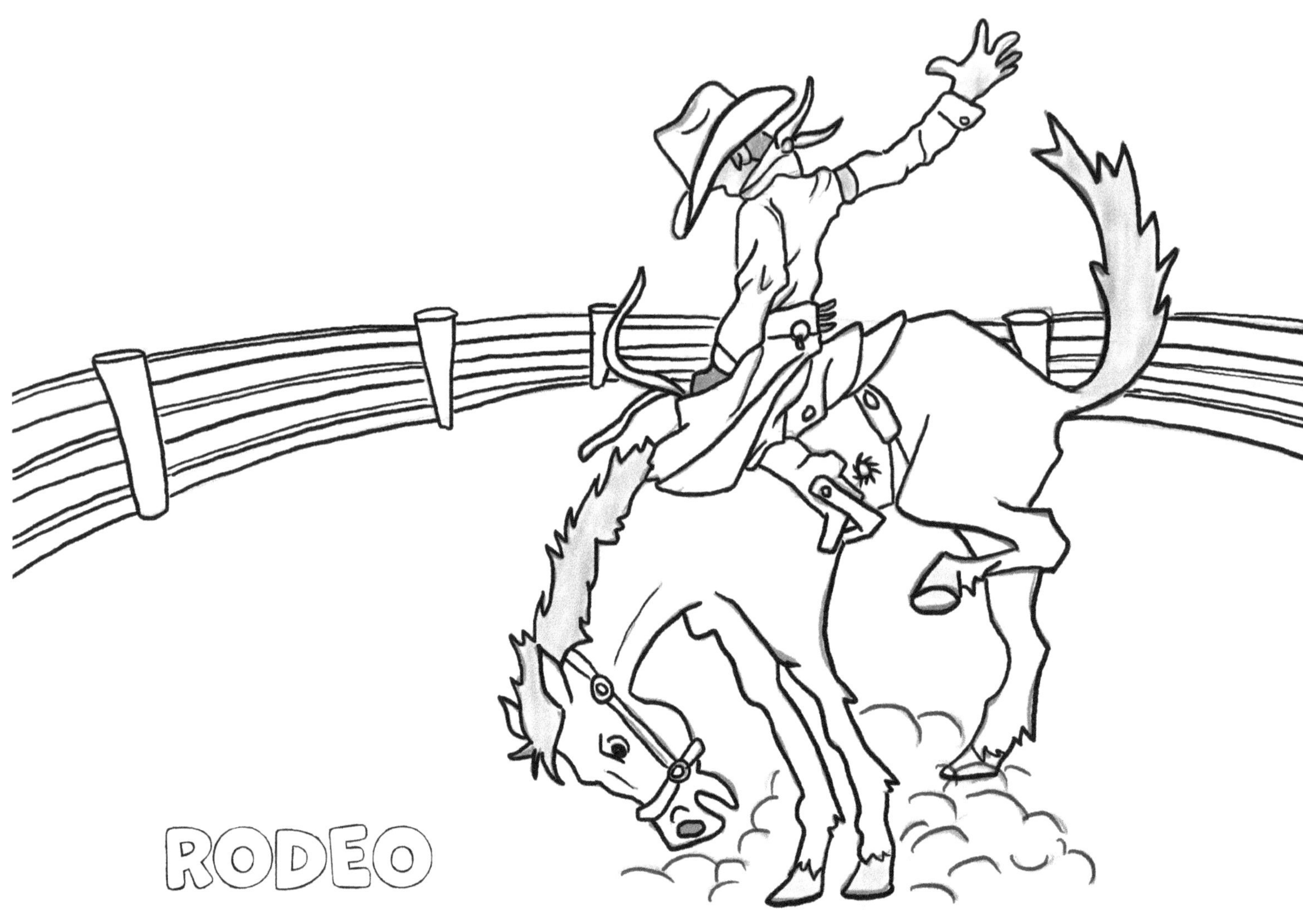

RODEO

The Jackson Hole Rodeo is a long tradition.
Events include bull riding, barrel racing, roping,
bucking broncos, and a sheep chase for kids.

SNOW SPORTS

When it's snowing get your boots, gloves, hat, neck warmer, snow pants, jacket and head to the mountain. Whether you ski or snowboard (or want to try both) this town is the best! Trails are perfect for the adventures to live life and feel wind in your face as you fly down the .ill/

TETON RANGE

You can't miss them! From many spots in and around town, you can see the gorgeous Teton Range which is part of the Rocky Mountains. Named by French Voyageurs, the highest peak called The Grand Teton is 13,770 feet. Climb it!

UNIQUE AIRPORT

The Jackson Hole Airport has a very 'unique' fun fact. When you take off and land at JAC, it is the only airport located inside a National Park – Grand Teton National Park

Just over the pass are Victor and Driggs, Idaho and Grand Targhee Mountain in Alta, Wyoming. Endless wilderness, back country exploring, ice caves, spelunking, golf courses, and rivers to fish are adventures over the pass.

WINTER

Winter is the coldest season here, when bears hibernate and elk come down to the valleys from the high country. It is time when families gather around the warm fire.

XTREME SPORTS

Jackson Hole is home to lots of extreme sports! From rock climbing to whitewater rafting, it's all extreme here. Corbet's Couloir is a 20foot cliff that skiers like to jump from at Jackson Hole Mountain Resort. What an extreme drop!

YELLOWSTONE

Yellowstone National Park is close to Jackson and the nation's first National Park.
Old Faithful is a cone geyser that erupts about every sixty minutes. After watching the
eruption walk the boardwalk which leads to the backside of Old Faithful and observe
all the other geysers and how their name matches their shape.
Watch out for erupting geysers as you walk around, sometimes they erupt and splash out
on the trails. Yellowstone has the thermal pools that are very colorful, and look around
carefully, there is wildlife everywhere!

ZZZZ

After a day as an adventurer in the
great outdoors, it's time to ZZZZ...
Tomorrow will be another day to explore!
As you fall asleep, think about the best
part of your adventures today–
it will be a treasured memory you will
never forget.